Lilian Bland

THE FIRST WOMAN IN THE WORLD
TO DESIGN, BUILD AND FLY AN AEROPLANE

by

Guy Warner

Founded 1968

Lilian Bland in her overalls (Flight Magazine)

Foreword

AT THE BLACKPOOL AVIATION Meeting in 1909 a woman was seen, carefully making notes and taking measurements of the aircraft on display. No doubt someone asked "Who is the secretive designer who has sent his secretary to collect all these details for him?" But there was no such secretive designer. Surprise, surprise, Lilian Bland was taking notes on her own behalf. Many people have looked enviously at birds, wishing they too had the ability to fly. Lilian Bland looked, and wished, and translated her wishes into reality. It is good to recall her achievements. In this booklet Guy Warner well describes the brief but significant flying career of a remarkable woman. He draws on the researches of others, notably Peter Lewis, a generation ago. One of Lilian's great-great-nieces is a light aircraft pilot, and she is married to a Boeing 747 Captain. What a long way flight has come in a hundred years. How much we owe to pioneers like Lilian, who shared their knowledge and experience with others.

Edward Pratt (The Rev.)
(Great-nephew of Lilian Bland)

Lilian Bland and the Mayfly (Flight Magazine)

Introduction

THE ACHIEVEMENTS OF Ulster's Harry Ferguson, the first man to fly an aeroplane in Ireland, on December 31, 1909, have quite rightly been celebrated. Yet how many know of the equally meritorious work of Lilian Bland – the first woman in the world, never mind Ireland, to design, build and fly her own aircraft? Indeed, has this been celebrated sufficiently in Carnmoney, where she constructed her biplane at Tobarcooran House in Glebe Road West? In this, the centenary year of Lilian Bland's pioneering flights, it is fitting that the Ulster Aviation Society is commemorating her technical skill, her determination to succeed and her bravery. The ancient village of Carnmoney has been part of Newtownabbey since 1958, as indeed have the villages of Whiteabbey and Whitehouse, which are also associated with this story. There is no doubt that Lilian Bland's name and deeds should be remembered when considering the contribution made by women to the development of aviation; a roll of honour which could include such personalities as Amy Johnson, Amelia Earhart, Harriet Quimby, Madame la Baronne de Laroche [i], Lady Mary Bailey, Lady Sophie Heath, Jean Batten, Diana Barnato Walker, Beryl Markham, Hanna Reitsch, Jacqueline Cochran, Sheila Scott and Polly Vacher, to name just a few.

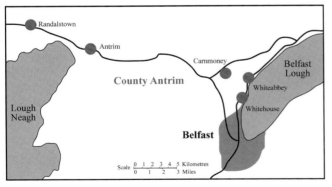

A portrait photograph of Lilian taken in 1907 (Ulster Aviation Society)

Lilian Bland's Story

Rev R.W. Bland from a miniature
(St George's Church and Rev Edward Pratt)

WHILE LILIAN EMILY BLAND was born at Willington House, near Maidstone in Kent on September 28, 1878, her family had deep roots in Ireland, Belfast and Whiteabbey. There had been Blands in Ireland since at least 1670 – the earliest name noted in Burke's Irish Family Records being Thomas Bland of Lisnagarvan, Co Down. Lilian's grandfather, the Reverend Robert Wintringham Bland MA, JP, was born in 1794 at Blandsfort in Queen's County (now Co Laois) which had been built by his grandfather, Colonel John Bland. Robert, who had studied at Trinity College, Dublin, had been the Perpetual Curate of Upper Falls at St George's Church in Belfast between 1825 and 1836, the oldest Anglican place of worship in the city. He returned to the church to conduct services and deliver a sermon from time to time until 1847. From 1845 to 1849 he was the District Curate of St John's Parish Church at Whitehouse, a few miles from the city, in Co Antrim on the north shore of Belfast Lough. With his wife, Alicia, who was from Dungannon, he raised a family of six children at Abbeyville in Whiteabbey, a mile or so along the coast from Whitehouse. He was also well known as a Justice of the Peace. From 1894 until his death in 1923 his second son, Major General Edward Loftus Bland, Royal Engineers, lived at Woodbank, which was adjacent to Abbeyville. Robert's eldest son, John Humphrey Bland, who was born in 1828, became an artist and owned Fernagh House, not far away from the family home. Between 1848 and 1861, having gained a BA at Trinity, he studied art in Paris at the École des Beaux-Arts and in the studios of François-Edouard Picot and Thomas Couture, exhibiting his work at the Royal

Academy in London and the Belfast Art Society. In 1867 he married Emily Charlotte Madden of Burgh Apton in Norfolk; they had three children, of whom Lilian was the youngest. When his wife became ill in 1900, John Humphrey brought his family back to Ireland where he set up home at Tobarcooran House with his sister, Mrs Sarah Smythe, the widow of General WJ Smythe RA, FRS, who had died in 1887. In time Emily became so ill that she had to live in a warmer climate, moving to the Mediterranean with her daughter, Eva, while Lilian and her father remained at Tobarcooran. Emily died in 1906.

Tobarcooran House (Carl Schwab via Mrs Norah Schwab)

Lilian had already made a name for herself as a journalist, both for local Irish papers and London magazines and as an acclaimed press photographer. She further astonished her contemporaries in Carnmoney and scandalised her aunt by wearing riding breeches, smoking cigarettes in public, tinkering with motor car engines and riding astride rather than sidesaddle. She was also one of the first ladies in Ireland to apply for a jockey's licence. Moreover, she was a crack shot and was not averse to lying in wait for poachers, before sending them and their lurchers packing with a well-aimed burst of shotgun pellets. All of these characteristics were sufficient to make her stand out anywhere in the British Isles during the Edwardian period, and rather more so in Presbyterian Ulster.

She had become interested in aviation through her hobby of photographing bird life; in particular she had become fascinated by the seagulls wheeling in the skies over the west coast of Scotland while she was staying with friends at Roshven near Kinlochmoidart in the summer of 1908. Later that year she exhibited, at the Royal Photographic Society in London, a selection of the colour photographs which she had produced, which she believed were the first colour plates of live birds to be taken. When, in the following year, Louis Blériot[ii] flew across the English Channel on July 25, her uncle Robert sent her a postcard of the Blériot XI monoplane, including a note of the machine's dimensions, her aviation ambitions were further kindled. She read all the books and magazine articles she could obtain about aeroplanes and flight – including the

Louis Blériot sets off across the English Channel on July 25, 1909 (Author's Collection)

The cover of the programme for Blackpool Aviation Week in October 1909. The event was organised by the Blackpool Corporation and the Lancashire Aero Club and had been inspired by the Champagne Flying Week at Rheims in August 1909, where the Mayor of Blackpool had been an enthusiastic spectator. It was subsequently reported, "The weather on the opening day was beautiful, the sky was clear and the ground was perfect. The first to make a start was AV Roe but his machine failed to lift off. Henry Farman brought out Paulhan's machine and he completed a circuit of the course to thunderous applause. Paulhan also made one circuit. Later in the day Farman thrilled the crowd with a very steady flight of nearly 14 miles, seven times round the aerodrome. 12,000 people took the opportunity to look at all the aeroplanes on the ground." (Blackpool International Airport)

weekly *Flight* magazine, which was first published in January 1909. Later that year she had the opportunity to visit the Blackpool Aviation Meeting, which was held from October 19-23 and was the first officially recognised air display to be held in the United Kingdom. She wrote a letter home to her father on October 20,

> I have seen them fly, and looked over all the flying machines; they are all made very much the same way and they looked smaller than I expected. After hours of waiting Latham brought his machine out and it started running along the field and then gradually rose and flew half a circuit, when its wings or skid caught in a ditch, and broke the skid and bent the propeller. Paulhan flew in a Farman machine, several rounds of the course and alighted quite gracefully ... in flying they keep their heads to the wind and turn a corner by drifting round tail-first ... the Gnome motor is the best. The few English machines are, I imagine, no good – much too small and fitted with motor-bike engines ... most of them are covered with tyre fabric, lashed on like lace boots sewn or tacked ... the wheels are on castors with small springs.

As can be judged from the above, Lilian was highly observant and by no means uncritical. She was not over-awed by either the magnificent men or their flying machines. She made a careful inspection of the aircraft, measuring and recording their dimensions, examining their structures, method of construction and engines. Many years later the Department of Aeronautical Engineering at Queen's University, Belfast, examined her notebooks and technical drawings and commented very favourably on her technical skills and grasp of the subject.

Back at Tobarcooran, Lilian made full use of the late General Smythe's well appointed workshop at the back of the house and constructed a model biplane glider with a wingspan of six feet, which flew successfully under tow. Satisfied with this proof of concept, during the winter of 1909-10 she designed and manufactured her

AV Roe with the Roe Triplane at Blackpool in 1909 (Blackpool International Airport)

Henri Farman (Philip Jarrett Collection)

Louis Paulhan (Philip Jarrett Collection)

Hubert Latham (Philip Jarrett Collection)

The coach-house at Tobarcooran in 2010 (G. Warner)

aeroplane from spruce, ash, elm and bamboo, covered with unbleached calico, which she doped with a home-mixed concoction of gelatine and formalin to make it waterproof. Lilian obtained the metal parts from Samuel Girvan of Ballyclare and the AV Roe Company in Manchester, which had itself been formed as recently as January 1, 1910. After the individual sections were made in the workroom, she carried them across to the coach-house, where the full-scale biplane glider was assembled. When finished it had a wingspan of 27 feet 7 inches. In December she wrote her first letter to *Flight* magazine, in which she discussed the possibility of taking-off in her glider using the skids in the manner of a toboggan on snow, the use of metal parts, the recipe for a good varnish to proof calico and the merits of ash instead of spruce. She finished her letter, "Hoping information may be of use." The Founder and Editor, Stanley Spooner, "a gentleman in the best sense of the word," commented as follows,

> It is at all times a pleasure to us to receive such a thoroughly helpful letter as the above, and the fact that it comes from a lady not only enhances the interest which attaches to it, but shows how far-reaching is the fascination of flight. We expect much from Ireland in aviation, as in every other phase of daring sport, and we cordially wish success to our correspondent.

Lilian decided to name her aeroplane the *Mayfly*. After the first tethered trial Lilian wrote to *Flight* magazine again, and her letter appeared in the issue of February 19, 1910,

MISS LILIAN E BLAND'S BIPLANE "MAYFLY"

I enclose two photos of my biplane, the "Mayfly." I made her entirely myself, with the exception of the metal clips, and, of course the sockets, strainers,

Testing the glider on Carnmoney Hill (From An Edwardian Echo by Peter Lewis)

etc., were bought from English firms. I think she is the first biplane made in Ireland.

I had her out again to-day, wind of 18 mph. My only difficulty is at present to prevent her flying when I do not want her to.

To-day I had three men to assist me, two of them knew nothing about it, and she ran the rope through their hands and soared up 20 ft before anyone was prepared. Fortunately the third man and myself had hold of a long rope, which saved the situation, in

Lilian Bland and the Mayfly on Carnmoney Hill (Flight and JM Bruce GS Leslie collection)

fact we got the machine soaring beautifully for some time until a down wind caught the elevators which I had fastened, when she dived down and broke both skids, but did no other damage. It is quite a new sensation being charged by an aeroplane.

We then had quite a lively time sailing her down hill to the shed; a 4 ft bank was cleared in fine style, and indeed the only drawback was the pace, (for she wants to go about 30 mph). I have now altered the steering arrangement so that the elevators can be controlled from the ground, which I naturally ought to have done from the first. I am also fitting two side panels, as I cannot very well work the balancing wings from the ground. I have not yet had a chance of ascertaining the gliding angle exactly, but she soars with vertical ropes, and I imagine her angle is about 7 degrees. As I told you, she rises straight off the ground when faced to the wind. If we bring her gliding down in a steady wind she lands as softly as a feather. A few hours work has made the skids stronger than they were before; they both broke where the wood was cross-grained, but I have the greatest difficulty here to get hold of good wood. The skids are American elm, which is very springy, and I must say they were severely tried.

Lilian E Bland

[Other aviators in embryo will not fail to have read with pleasure Miss Bland's breezy letter of her preliminary experiments nor to wish her success in all future trials, particularly when she becomes the pilot of her machine – Ed]

Flight magazine was the "internet chatroom" or "networking website" of its day, where pioneer aviators could report on the success or otherwise of their endeavours, exchange ideas and experiences and pick up useful hints and tips.

Throughout that spring of 1910 the *Mayfly* was flown as a glider on the slopes of Carnmoney Hill, a volcanic neck or plug which rises to a height of 785 feet above sea level. Lilian's chief assistant was her aunt's gardener's "boy", Joe Blain. Joe by that time was 32 years old and was essentially an outdoors man who loved shooting and other sports. He was also an early exponent of the new-fangled bicycling craze.

Subsequently, four stalwart members of the Royal Irish Constabulary also gave a hand. Their job was to hold on to the glider after the initial series of tethered flights had been successfully accomplished by Lilian and Joe. The lifting qualities of the *Mayfly* were so good that the four constables were in danger of becoming test pilots, so they released their hold with great alacrity, leaving Joe Blain to cling

Joe Blain with his shooting trophy and gold medal (via Bombardier Belfast)

Aunt Sarah at the controls of the glider (From An Edwardian Echo by Peter Lewis)

Sam Girvan & Joe Blain on Carnmoney Hill with the Mayfly (Flight Magazine and JM Bruce GS Leslie collection)

The Mayfly with engine installed (Flight Magazine)

on, turn the glider out of wind and bring it back to earth. Before and after the flight trials the glider was stored in a nearby shed beside the quarry belonging to Mr Tom Smith.

Convinced by the demonstration that she was on the right path, Lilian Bland then wrote to the aviation pioneer and nascent manufacturer, AV Roe[iii], asking if he could supply her with an Edwards/Avro two-stroke, air-cooled engine. He agreed to make or source a suitable engine at a cost of £100. In the meantime Lilian carried out further research in the observation of the flow of air over lifting surfaces, by the simple expedient of passing the aerofoil shapes through her steam-filled bathroom. In July she caught the ferry to England and returned with a 20 hp engine and propeller. Two other passengers on the boat train asked the purpose of her baggage – "To make an aeroplane." she replied, "What is an aeroplane?" was the response. The engine was test run with the aid of a whiskey bottle filled with petrol and her aunt's ear trumpet. An engine mounting was added to the trailing edge of the lower wing, a seat made from a remnant of carpet was furnished for the leading edge, a proper petrol tank arrived, a T-bar control yoke was fitted and a tricycle undercarriage was constructed. The *Mayfly* was configured as a pusher with the engine behind the pilot. Joe Blain started the engine by standing between the tailbooms and swinging the propeller; not a task for the faint-hearted, as Lilian noted, "It was not a good engine, a beast to start and it got too hot." But once it was coaxed into action it ran satisfactorily enough.

The small field at Carnmoney was judged to be inadequate for flight trials. Instead, Lord O'Neill's 800-acre park at Randalstown was made available and a hut was put up. Small wheels were fitted to the skids, while the front and rear booms were removed, which enabled the *Mayfly* to be towed to its new location and then re-erected. The field also apparently was home to a bull, which, as Lilian wrote to *Flight*, "If it gets annoyed and charges I shall have every inducement to fly!" When the weather was suitable – calm with little or no wind – Joe and Lilian would cycle the twelve miles over to

The Mayfly in the field near Randalstown in 1910 (from An Edwardian Echo by Peter Lewis)

Randalstown. The first tentative hops were made in August 1910. At first the aviatrix could scarcely believe that she had left the ground until viewing the evidence – the cessation and resumption of the wheel tracks which denoted her flightpath. The flights increased in length to nearly a quarter of a mile, and the *Belfast Evening Telegraph* declared on September 7,

Joe Blain with the Mayfly (Ulster Aviation Society)

First Irish Biplane to Fly.
Co Antrim Lady's Successes in Aviation.

Miss Bland of Carnmoney, Co Antrim, who is the first lady to design and construct an aeroplane, has been making short flights with her machine near Randalstown. The biplane was first tested as a glider, and proved so successful that Miss Bland decided to fit it with a motor. Since the aeroplane has been on its flying ground the weather has been most unfavourable but the machine at its first trial rose

The Mayfly with its new rectangular rudder (From An Edwardian Echo by Peter Lewis)

Lilian checks the throttle (from An Edwardian Echo by Peter Lewis)

from the ground after a run of thirty feet and flew for some distance a few feet above the ground. The machine is built somewhat on the lines of a Curtiss biplane but has two elevators working separately or together in connection with the horizontal tailplanes. The machine carries over 2lb per square foot, and weighs, with the pilot, under 600lbs. The motor is a 20 hp Avro, two-cylinder opposed type and has so far proved most satisfactory and reliable.

The article included two photographs showing the whole aircraft and a close-up view of the motor and propeller, captioned "Miss Bland's Biplane" and "The Motor and Propeller. The engine is mounted half-way between the planes [wings]."

Further letters and photographs appeared at regular intervals in *Flight*, culminating in a major three-page article, written by Lilian herself, in the December 17, 1910 issue, which also included a scale drawing of the aeroplane and detailed sketches of technical details. She compared the skills required when flying an aeroplane with those which also came in handy when hunting on horseback.

> When the engine starts, the draught from the propeller lifts the tail and the tip of the skids off the ground, and the machine balances on the two wheels; the third wheel in front only comes into action over rough ground, and to prevent the machine from going on her nose; it answers the purpose admirably, as my practice ground is rough grass with ridge and furrow, which on hunting principles I take at a slant.

Lilian concluded her article with the following very sensible observations,

> I should not advise any amateurs to commence building aeroplanes unless they have plenty of spare time and money, but there are nevertheless many people who like myself have the time, but lack the necessary £.s.d. As a result of my experience I am certain that the only way to build an aeroplane cheaply is to put the best of everything into it. One can learn a great deal by watching good pilots. Unfortunately we have none in Ireland at present[iv], but I have been fortunate in seeing Farman[v], Paulhan[vi] and Latham[vii], all masters of the art.

> To sum up the various points one has to settle before starting the construction of a machine:-

> Firstly – A place to fly it in. Bad ground is a waste of time and takes much longer to learn on.

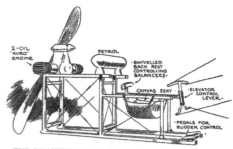

THE "MAYFLY."—Sketch showing the general arrangements of the detachable framework containing the power plant, &c.

The "Mayfly."—Detailed sketch of the outrigger pivot.

The sketches of technical details which featured in Flight Magazine on 17th December 1910.

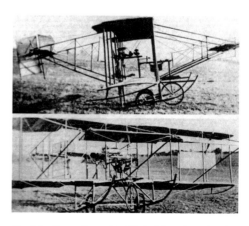

The Mayfly as pictured in Flight Magazine of 17th December 1910 (Flight Magazine)

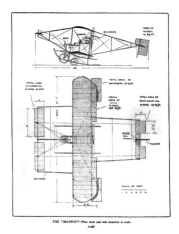

Mayfly plan from Flight magazine 1910

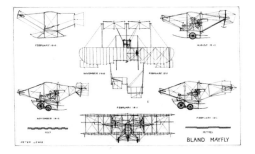

How the Mayfly's design progressed (An Edwardian Echo by Peter Lewis

Quarter scale model at Carnmoney March 1911 (Flight Magazine)

Secondly – The engine, if it is of low hp, the aeroplane must be light and have a large area to weight.

Thirdly – The placing of engine and pilot and whether main planes will carry all the weight &c.

Fourthly – To draw out every detail to scale, and if trying an original design, to make a good-sized model, and see if any new point in controls or design is going to work as intended.

Fifthly – Design the machine so that it can be easily taken to pieces for transport, &c. (by turning the skids round, my machine will wheel along any road when the outriggers are taken off).

In conclusion … the engine and propeller must be reasonably efficient, otherwise it is only a waste of time.

She had plans to improve the design, and built a quarter-scale model of this, as well as inserting an advert in *Flight* early in 1911:

Both Lilian Bland and Harry Ferguson turned their back on aviation after these achievements. Neither attempted to gain Aviators'

Certificates issued by the Royal Aero Club. Harry Ferguson became world-famous as the inventor of the three-point linkage and in the field of automotive design and production, particularly tractors, while, in 1911 Lilian was bribed by the offer of a motor car from her elderly father to pursue less hazardous activities. She collected the car, a 20 hp Model T Ford, in Dublin and halfway back to Belfast took her first and only driving lesson. She then set up a sub-agency in Belfast selling Fords, which was announced in *Flight* and brought down further ire from her aunt, as being most unladylike. More shocks were to come as, in October, Lilian married her cousin, Lieutenant Charles Loftus Bland, formerly of the Royal Artillery and the son of Major General Edward Loftus Bland RE of Woodbank. In the December 23, 1911 issue, *Flight* wished the couple well and noted that Charles had read of his cousin's exploits in the magazine and had come to the conclusion that she would be a suitable bride to tackle the pioneer life. Charles had become a lumberjack in Canada, and Lilian joined him there in April 1912 to carve out a new life in establishing a farm on 160 acres of land at Quatsino Sound, Vancouver Island, in British Columbia. They had a daughter, Pat, who tragically died in 1929 at the age of 16, after contracting tetanus following an accident. Aunt Sarah had died in 1917 at the age of 85, while Lilian's father, John Humphrey, had passed away in 1919 at the age of 91. Lilian returned to England alone in 1935, to live with her brother, Captain Robert Bland R Irish Rifles, at Penshurst in Kent. In 1965 she told the *New York Times*,

> When I came back from Canada I became a gardener. I gambled my wages on the stock market and was very lucky. I made enough to come here [Sennen in Cornwall] ten years ago. I now spend my time painting, gardening and gambling a little.

Lilian Bland died on May 11, 1971 at the age of 92, and is buried in the churchyard of the village of Sennen, near Land's End in Cornwall. Joe Blain married in May 1914 and had four daughters. He died on March 3, 1955.

On Tuesday 31st August 2010 Kate Welsh laid a wreath on behalf of the Ulster Aviation Society on Lilian's grave in the churchyard at Sennen in Cornwall. Lilian's great nephew, the Rev Edward Pratt laid a floral tribute on behalf of the family. At the same time Mark Hiller and Glen Corcoran of MSH Flight Training, Lands End Airport flew over in salute at a height of 500 feet. Ted Pratt later wrote, "I thought how appropriate it was for the fly-past to be conducted by light aircraft, like Lilian's Mayfly."

It is an odd but true fact that Lilian's exploits were more widely known 40 or 50 years ago than is the case today. It is quite remarkable how in this the centenary year of her pioneering flights, just how many people there are who have heard of Harry Ferguson but who know nothing of Lilian Bland. In 1964 a very readable article about her appeared in the company journal *Shorts Quarterly Review*; this was reproduced shortly afterwards in the *Ulster Commentary*. In the same year Peter Lewis wrote about *Lilian Bland and the Mayfly* for *Flight* magazine. He later followed this up by writing a much longer and more detailed account which he titled *An Edwardian Echo* and which featured in the book *Aircraft 1973*,

SHORT   BROTHERS   &   HARLAND   LIMITED

P.O. BOX 241
QUEEN'S ISLAND BELFAST 3

LONDON OFFICE:
BERKELEY SQUARE HOUSE
BERKELEY SQUARE W1
Telephone: MAYfair 9541

Telegrams: AIRCRAFT BELFAST
Telephone: BELFAST 58444
Telex: 74-539

HGC/NGC/10519   5th May, 1964

Mrs. Lilian Bland,
Sennen,
Lands End,
CORNWALL

Dear Mrs. Bland,

I can at last send you photocopies of the local paper dealing with Harry Ferguson's first flight and then yours. You will see that you were the first biplane but that he was the first aeroplane proper. At any rate you must have been the first woman in the world to build and fly an aeroplane, which isn't so bad.

Yours sincerely,

H.G. Conway

Encl:

In 1964 Lilian Bland corresponded with Hugh Conway, the Managing Director of Short Brothers & Harland Limited

published by Ian Allan. Further brief mentions were made in three general Irish aviation histories by John Corlett, Liam Byrne and Donal MacCarron between 1980 and 2000. In the early 1990s there was a tentative plan to make a feature film of Lilian's life but sadly this did not come to fruition. The Ulster History Circle raised a Blue Plaque in memory of Lilian in 1997 and placed it on the former site of Tobarcooran House, but it is not readily accessible to the public. Woodbank is owned by the renowned sculptor, John Sherlock and his wife, Rosemary and retains many of the original features from Lilian's time. The coach-house, in which John believes Lilian may have constructed some of her aeroplane, has been converted to self-catering holiday accomodation. Both Abbeyville and Fernagh House have long since been demolished. In 2003, as part of its celebration of the Centenary of Flight, An Post in the Irish Republic issued a set of four postage stamps, one of which featured Lilian and the Mayfly. It is to be hoped, therefore, that this publication and other commemorative efforts by the Ulster Aviation Society, Newtownabbey Borough Council and the Randalstown Historical Society (which on August 31, 2010 raised a plaque to Lilian at Station House, Shane's Castle) will stimulate interest in the life and achievements of this remarkable woman.

Lilian Bland Stamp (An Post)

Lilian in flight in February 1911 (Flight magazine)

Notes

Madame la Baronne de Laroche (Author's Collection)

Hilda Hewlett (Brooklands Museum)

The engine displayed at Brooklands Museum (Julian Temple)

i   Madame la Baronne de Laroche (1886–1919), whose real name was Elise Raymonde Deroche, was the first woman in the world to gain a pilot's certificate, in France on March 8, 1910. The first woman in Britain to qualify for the Royal Aero Club Aviators' Certificate was Hilda Beatrice Hewlett (1864–1943), who won her "ticket" flying a Farman biplane on August 29, 1911, at Brooklands.

ii   Louis Blériot (1872–1936) made his fortune as an engineer with a design for motor car headlamps. He began experimenting with flying machines at the turn of the century. His first really successful aeroplane was the Blériot XI of 1909, with which he won the £1000 prize for the first crossing of the English Channel by an aeroplane, which he completed in 37 minutes. After 50 crashes and many injuries, he gave up flying and became a successful aircraft manufacturer.

iii   Alliott Verdon Roe (1877–1958) was one of the foremost pioneers of British aviation. He possibly made his first short flight in an aeroplane of his own construction in June 1908, though this is disputed by modern historians. AV Roe & Co was founded in 1910, and its most famous product was the Avro 504, one of the great aircraft in the history of aviation. It is believed that Lilian sold the engine to the young Sidney Camm, who would later go on to design many famous Hawker aircraft. This engine is now on display at the Brooklands Museum in Weybridge, Surrey – though some historians question its provenance.

iv   No good pilots in Ireland – it is believed that Lilian did not see eye to eye with Harry Ferguson, whom she regarded as being less than generous in sharing his empirical aviation knowledge with others.

v   Henry Farman (1874–1958) was born of English parents living in France. During 1908 he was France's premier flyer. In 1909 he set up his own aeroplane factory, joining forces with his brother, Maurice, in 1912. Many successful types were constructed by the Farman company, including the famous "Shorthorns" and "Longhorns", which were used as trainers in the First World War.

vi   Louis Paulhan (1883–1963) served in the French Army balloon corps before teaching himself to fly in 1909. In 1910 he won a prize of $10,000 for a long-distance flight in California and then achieved victory in the epic *Daily Mail* London to Manchester air race. From 1916 to 1918 he served as a fighter pilot.

vii   Hubert Latham (1883–1912) was an Englishman who lived mostly in France. He hoped to beat Blériot in the race to be the first to fly the Channel but suffered engine problems when only a few miles from the English coast. On July 16, 1912, while on safari in Africa, he was charged by a wild buffalo and gored to death.

Reproduction of material from *Flight* Magazine is by kind permission of the Editor.
See also: (http://www.flightglobal.com/pdfarchive/)

Grateful thanks should also go to Julian Temple, the Curator of Aviation at the Brooklands Museum, to the aviation consultant, Philip Jarrett, to Dave Mallalieu and to Sue Kendrick of Blackpool International Airport. Thanks also to my good friends Ernie Cromie for his encouragement and proof-reading and to Graham Mehaffy for the map on page five. As always the input and skill of the team at Nicholson & Bass is much appreciated.

Guy Warner is a retired schoolteacher who grew up in Newtownabbey, he now lives in Greenisland with his wife Lynda. He is the author of more than a dozen books on aviation and has written a large number of articles for magazines in the UK, Ireland and the USA. He is a committee member of the Ulster Aviation Society – for more information about the Society please see www.ulsteraviationsociety.org.

Founded 1968